"Brad Jacobs: A Maverick's Journey"

Once upon a time, in the quaint city of Providence, Rhode Island, a boy named Brad Jacobs was born into a world of glittering jewels and global commerce. His father, a savvy fashion jewelry importer, and his mother, Charlotte Sybil, created a home where the air buzzed with discussions of markets and aesthetics. Young Brad, born on August 3, 1956, was a curious blend of his environment - a mind attuned to the beauty of art and the rhythm of numbers.

Brad's youth unfurled in the halls of Northfield Mount Hermon School, where he danced with melodies and equations, his mind always racing ahead, eager to explore beyond the conventional paths. College called to him, first Bennington and then Brown University, where music and mathematics were his chosen companions. But in 1976, the real world, vast and untamed, beckoned, and Brad, in a move that would define the rest of his life, left his textbooks behind.

The world of oil trading was his first arena. Here, in the bustling markets, Brad's entrepreneurial spirit took flight. By 1979, he had co-founded Amerex Oil Associates Inc., a testament to his nascent business acumen. The company's journey was a whirlwind of success, with Brad at its helm until its sale in 1983. But his ambitions were not to be tethered.

London called next, and Brad answered, founding Hamilton Resources Ltd. Amid the city's fog and grandeur, he navigated the intricate world of oil deals, honing his strategic mind. Yet, the pull of his homeland was strong, and in 1989, Brad returned to the States, planting the seeds of a venture that would redefine an industry.

United Waste Systems was born out of a simple yet revolutionary idea - consolidating small waste management companies to create a cohesive, efficient network. Brad's vision transformed into reality, and in 1992, he propelled the company into the public eye, culminating in a lucrative sale that echoed in the annals of business history.

The turn of the century saw Brad orchestrating another masterstroke with United Rentals. Like a skilled conductor, he led the company through a symphony of growth and expansion, establishing it as a juggernaut in the equipment rental sector.

But the crowning jewel of Brad's career was yet to come. In 2010, Jacobs Private Equity LLC marked the beginning of a singular focus - a focus that found its target in XPO Logistics. With a strategic investment, Brad reshaped the company, guiding it to become a titan of transportation and logistics. The spin-offs, GXO Logistics and RXO, were but stars in the galaxy he created.

Brad's life, however, was more than a relentless pursuit of business success. He found harmony in his personal life with Lamia, his partner, with whom he raised four children in their Greenwich home. Their abode, a sanctuary of art and love, housed masterpieces that whispered stories of Picasso and Calder, mirroring Brad's own journey of creativity and vision.

As the years unfurled, Brad, now a sage in the world of business, turned to sharing his wisdom. His upcoming book, "How to Make a Few Billion Dollars," promised to be a treasure trove of insights, a guide for those who dared to dream as he did.

Brad Jacobs' story is not just a chronicle of business conquests; it is a tale of a maverick who dared to chart his own course, a man who wove his dreams into the fabric of reality. In the storybook of American business legends, Brad's chapter is one of audacity, ingenuity, and the relentless pursuit of excellence - a true inspiration for every aspiring entrepreneur who looks up at the stars and dreams.

As the twilight of his career approached, Brad Jacobs, ever the visionary, began to look beyond the horizon of his vast business empire. His life, a tapestry of bold moves and strategic mastery, had been a whirlwind of activity, but now, he sought to impart the wisdom gleaned from his remarkable journey.

"How to Make a Few Billion Dollars," the book that he had poured his heart and soul into, was more than just a memoir or a business manual. It was a beacon, a guiding light for those who aspired to leave an indelible mark on the world. In its pages, Brad distilled the essence of his experiences, sharing not just strategies but also the philosophy that had powered his journey – a blend of relentless pursuit, adaptive thinking, and the courage to defy conventions.

Meanwhile, in the leafy, serene lanes of Greenwich, Connecticut, Brad's home was a reflection of his life's journey. Here, amidst the masterpieces of the greatest artists, he found peace and inspiration. His family, his anchor through the tumultuous waves of business, was a source of joy and pride. Brad's conversations with his children often sparkled with the same innovative spirit that had defined his career. In these dialogues, he passed on not just knowledge but a mindset - to question, to dream, and to dare.

As news of his book spread, the business world buzzed with anticipation. Here was a man who had not just witnessed but shaped the very dynamics of multiple industries. From the intricacies of oil trading in London to the complexities of logistics and waste management in the United States, Brad had navigated diverse terrains with unparalleled success. His insights were not just strategies but stories of challenges embraced and obstacles overcome.

In boardrooms and universities, among entrepreneurs and veterans of industry, Brad's upcoming book became a topic of eager discussion. What secrets did this titan of industry hold? What lessons could be learned from a man who had built empires, not once but repeatedly? The anticipation was not just about financial strategies; it was about understanding the ethos of a man who had repeatedly turned visions into realities.

As the release date neared, Brad found himself reflecting on his journey. The young boy from Providence who loved music and mathematics had traversed a path filled with risks and rewards. Each decision, each turn he took was a note in the symphony of his life, culminating in a crescendo that resonated with success and fulfillment.

Brad Jacobs' story was not just about building businesses; it was about building a legacy. It was a narrative of how passion, when coupled with perseverance and foresight, can sculpt a life that is not only successful but also meaningful. His journey stood as a testament to the belief that with the right mindset, every challenge is an opportunity, and every dream, no matter how audacious, is achievable.

In the tranquility of his study, surrounded by the silent whispers of the art that adorned his walls, Brad Jacobs penned the final words of his book. It was more than a closing chapter; it was an invitation to the next generation of dreamers and doers to embark on their own extraordinary journeys.

As Brad Jacobs set the pen down, the last sentence of his book echoing in his mind, he felt a profound sense of accomplishment and anticipation. The journey of penning "How to Make a Few Billion Dollars" had been cathartic and enlightening, a reflection of his own life's path, strewn with both triumphs and trials.

In the quietude of his study, he pondered over the young entrepreneurs who would turn the pages of his book. He imagined their fiery spirits and hungry minds, eager to carve their niches in the world. Brad knew that his words would ignite in them the same spark that had driven him all those years ago - a spark that could light the fire of innovation and ambition.

His thoughts wandered to the early days of his career, the risks he had taken, and the relentless drive that had propelled him. These memories were now immortalized in his book, a legacy that would outlive him. He hoped that his story would be a lighthouse for those navigating the often tumultuous waters of entrepreneurship.

The art in his home, each piece a narrative of genius and creativity, now seemed to resonate with his own life story. From Picasso's bold strokes to Calder's dynamic sculptures, each piece was a testament to the power of vision and the courage to break new ground. Brad felt a kinship with these artists, a shared journey of creating something enduring and impactful.

As the launch date of the book neared, Brad's life took on a rhythm marked by interviews and speaking engagements. Each interaction was an opportunity to share his philosophy - that success is not just about financial gain but about making a meaningful impact, about building something that stands the test of time.

In these interactions, Brad often shared personal anecdotes, lessons he had learned not just in boardrooms but in life. He spoke of the importance of balance, of finding joy in the journey, and of the immense value of relationships, both personal and professional. His insights went beyond business strategies; they touched upon the essence of a fulfilled life.

Back in Greenwich, amidst the laughter and love of his family, Brad found his greatest joy and peace. His children, now embarking on their own journeys, were a living testament to the values he had instilled - the courage to dream, the perseverance to pursue those dreams, and the integrity to do it right.

As Brad Jacobs looked out from his study window, his gaze falling on the serene landscape that had been witness to his most profound moments of reflection, he felt a deep sense of gratitude. His journey had been extraordinary, marked by bold decisions and transformative actions. But more than that, it had been a journey of growth, learning, and giving back.

"How to Make a Few Billion Dollars" was now ready to make its way into the world, a beacon of knowledge and inspiration. But for Brad, it was more than just a book. It was a chapter of his life, an invitation to others to dream big and a reminder that with hard work, vision, and a bit of daring, anything is possible.

In the tranquil twilight of his career, Brad Jacobs had not only built a legacy of business achievements but had also sown the seeds for future generations to grow their dreams. His story, a blend of business acumen and personal ethos, would continue to inspire and guide aspiring entrepreneurs, echoing his belief that in the grand tapestry of life, each one of us has the power to weave our own extraordinary story.

As the release of "How to Make a Few Billion Dollars" approached, Brad Jacobs found himself in a whirlwind of anticipation and reflection. The world awaited his book not just as a business guide, but as a window into the mind of a man who had reshaped industries and created monumental success from the ground up.

Brad's days were filled with a flurry of activity. Interviews and speaking engagements lined up, each providing a platform to share his journey and insights. But amidst this busyness, Brad remained grounded, his thoughts often drifting to his humble beginnings in Providence, Rhode Island. It was this grounding that he hoped to pass on through his book – the understanding that great success often starts with small, determined steps.

In Greenwich, his home was abuzz with excitement. Lamia, his wife, shared his joy and pride, her support unwavering as it had been throughout their life together. Their children, each charting their own course, looked to their father not just as a business icon but as a role model who balanced professional ambition with personal integrity and family values.

As he interacted with young entrepreneurs and business students, Brad felt a profound sense of responsibility. He saw in their eyes the same spark that had driven him, and he knew that his words could help fan those flames. He emphasized the importance of adaptability, ethical leadership, and the relentless pursuit of innovation. His message was clear: success is not just about what you achieve, but how you achieve it.

The art that adorned the walls of his home, once silent witnesses to his relentless work and deep contemplations, now seemed to share in the celebratory mood. The artworks, each with a unique story, were like milestones of his journey, reminding him of the different phases of his life and career.

As the book hit the shelves, it was met with enthusiasm and acclaim. Readers were captivated not only by Brad's business strategies but also by his personal philosophy and life lessons. The book quickly became a must-read for anyone aspiring to make a mark in the business world, praised for its straightforward, insightful, and inspiring content.

In the heart of Greenwich, at a quiet and intimate book launch event, Brad stood surrounded by family, friends, and long-time colleagues. He felt a surge of emotions as he reflected on the journey that had led him here. His speech was heartfelt, expressing gratitude and hope for the future. He spoke of the importance of leaving a positive imprint on the world, of building something larger than oneself.

As Brad signed copies of his book, he looked into the eyes of each person he met. In these moments, he saw the impact of his work, the transfer of knowledge and inspiration to another generation of dreamers and doers. Each handshake, each smile, was a connection, a shared understanding of the relentless pursuit of excellence and the courage to dream big.

In the evenings, Brad would sit in his study, sometimes glancing at the first copy of his book that sat proudly on his shelf. He knew that the true measure of its success wouldn't be in sales numbers, but in the lives and careers it shaped, in the businesses and innovations it inspired.

Brad Jacobs' story, from a music and mathematics-loving student to a renowned business mogul, was a testament to the power of vision, grit, and resilience. His journey was more than a series of business ventures; it was a narrative of transformation and impact, a legacy etched not just in the annals of business history, but in the hearts and minds of those he inspired. And as each day passed, Brad looked forward with optimism, ready to embrace whatever new chapters life had in store, knowing that his story, his lessons, would continue to inspire and guide future generations in their quest to weave their own extraordinary tales.

As the sun set on another day, Brad Jacobs sat in his study, the fading light casting long shadows across the room filled with memories of a lifetime. The success of his book had surpassed even his own expectations, becoming a beacon for aspiring entrepreneurs worldwide. But for Brad, the true reward lay in the ripple effect of his experiences, the way his story resonated with others, inspiring them to pursue their dreams with vigor and integrity.

With the book now part of his legacy, Brad found more time to engage in personal pursuits that had taken a back seat during his relentless career. He returned to his love for music, the melodies and harmonies offering a soothing contrast to the high-stakes world of business. Mathematics, with its elegant solutions and logical rigor, still fascinated him, providing a mental sanctuary that was both challenging and comforting.

Brad's involvement in the business world, though less hands-on, remained impactful. He became a sought-after mentor and advisor, his insights and experiences invaluable to those navigating the complexities of the business landscape. He often visited universities and business forums, sharing his knowledge and nurturing the next generation of leaders.

His philanthropic efforts, always a part of his life, now took on greater significance. Brad and Lamia dedicated more time and resources to various causes, focusing on education, environmental conservation, and the arts. Their philanthropy was not just about donations but about making a tangible difference, about empowering communities and fostering sustainable change.

In Greenwich, their home was often filled with the laughter and chatter of their children and grandchildren. These moments were Brad's greatest treasures, a reminder that his most important legacy was the love and unity of his family. The values he had instilled in his children were now being passed on to another generation, a continuous thread weaving through the fabric of their family history.

Brad also found joy in his art collection, each piece a friend with its own story. He often walked through his collection, pausing to admire a de Kooning or a Calder, each a reminder of the beauty and creativity that humanity could achieve. He mused on the parallels between art and business – both required vision, courage, and the ability to see beyond the obvious.

As he gazed out of his study window, Brad reflected on the winding path his life had taken. From a young man passionate about music and mathematics to a business titan who had reshaped industries, his journey was a tapestry of bold decisions, relentless pursuit of excellence, and an unwavering commitment to his values. His story was a testament to the belief that with hard work, vision, and a dash of daring, one could indeed make a few billion dollars, and more importantly, make a difference in the world.

In the tranquility of his later years, Brad Jacobs found a deep sense of fulfillment. He had not only built businesses but had also built lives, not just created wealth but also created value. His journey, chronicled in his book and etched in the lives he touched, would continue to inspire and guide. Brad Jacobs' legacy was not just in the empires he built, but in the wisdom he imparted, the lives he enriched, and the paths he illuminated for those who dared to dream big and tread their own extraordinary journeys.

As the seasons changed, so did the rhythm of Brad Jacobs' life, settling into a pace that allowed for introspection and a broader view of his impact on the world. The businessman, once known for his relentless drive and laser-focused vision, was now embracing a role as a wise elder statesman in the business community, a beacon for those navigating the often-turbulent waters of entrepreneurship.

In his quieter moments, Brad found solace in the memories of his earlier, more tumultuous years. He often sat in his favorite armchair, a cup of coffee in hand, gazing out over the sprawling gardens of his Greenwich estate. These reflective moments were not just about reminiscing; they were about understanding the lessons of the past and envisioning how they could be applied to the future.

Brad's influence extended beyond the boardrooms and business seminars. He became a patron of the arts, recognizing the profound impact that creative expression had on society. His support helped nurture budding artists and brought diverse artworks to the public, fostering a culture of appreciation and understanding.

His commitment to environmental causes grew stronger with each passing year. Brad understood that his legacy was intertwined with the health of the planet, and he dedicated significant resources to initiatives aimed at conservation and sustainability. His efforts went beyond mere funding; he actively participated in policy discussions and advocacy, leveraging his influence for the greater good.

The Jacobs family, always close-knit, became even more so. Brad and Lamia's home was a hub of activity, with family gatherings, celebrations, and impromptu visits. Brad took great joy in mentoring his grandchildren, sharing stories of his adventures in business and life, instilling in them the same values of hard work, integrity, and the importance of giving back.

As his book continued to inspire the next generation of entrepreneurs, Brad often received letters and emails from readers. They wrote of how his story had motivated them to pursue their passions, to face challenges head-on, and to build businesses with a conscience. These messages were a source of great satisfaction to Brad, reaffirming that his journey had a purpose beyond his own achievements.

Despite stepping back from the day-to-day grind of business, Brad remained a figure of immense influence. His advice was sought by leaders in various fields, from young startup founders to seasoned CEOs. His insights, born of decades of experience, were as relevant as ever, reflecting a deep understanding of the ever-evolving business landscape.

In his later years, Brad often found himself reflecting on the concept of legacy. He had come to realize that true legacy was not about buildings named in one's honor or the accumulation of wealth and accolades. Instead, it was about the lives he had touched, the positive changes he had spurred in the world, and the continuation of his values through his family and those he had mentored.

As Brad Jacobs looked out into the twilight of his years, he saw not an ending, but a continuation. His journey had been one of transformation and growth, of challenges met and overcome, and of a relentless pursuit of a vision that extended far beyond himself. His story, woven into the fabric of countless other stories, would live on, a testament to the enduring power of dreaming big, working hard, and living with purpose and integrity. In the quiet of his study, surrounded by the symbols of his journey, Brad Jacobs smiled, content in the knowledge that his legacy would endure, inspiring and guiding future generations to build their own paths toward success and fulfillment.

As twilight gave way to the gentle embrace of night, Brad Jacobs remained in his study, surrounded by the tranquil silence that only the end of a day can bring. The soft glow of the lamp illuminated the room, casting a warm light on the shelves lined with books, each a repository of knowledge and adventure.

In these moments of solitude, Brad often thought about the concept of time - how it had been both a relentless pursuer and a generous ally throughout his journey. He pondered the countless decisions he had made, the risks he had taken, and the opportunities he had seized, each a stitch in the intricate tapestry of his life.

Outside, the stars began to twinkle in the clear night sky, a reminder of the vastness of the universe and the fleeting nature of human endeavors. Yet, in this vastness, Brad found not insignificance, but inspiration. He saw his life as part of a greater whole, a contribution to a story much larger than his own.

His thoughts often wandered to the future, to the world his grandchildren would inherit. He hoped that his actions, both in business and in his personal life, had helped shape a better, more sustainable world for them. The thought of his grandchildren growing up in a world rich in opportunities, filled with beauty and wonder, gave him a sense of peace.

Brad's philanthropic efforts, once a part of his business strategy, had evolved into a deeply personal mission. He focused on creating lasting impact, on projects that would not only provide immediate relief but also pave the way for long-term sustainability. Education, particularly in underserved communities, had become a passion project for him, driven by his belief in its power to transform lives.

As the night deepened, Brad's wife, Lamia, joined him in the study. Together, they reflected on the journey they had shared, the ups and downs, the triumphs and challenges. Lamia had been more than a partner; she had been a confidante, a source of strength and wisdom. Their conversation drifted from family to art, from business to the books they were reading, a testament to the rich tapestry of their shared experiences.

The couple often discussed their legacy, what they would leave behind for their children, their community, and the world. For Brad, it was clear that his greatest legacy would not be measured in financial terms but in the values he had upheld and passed on - integrity, hard work, compassion, and the unwavering belief in the potential of every individual.

As the clock struck midnight, Brad and Lamia decided to call it a night. They walked together, hand in hand, through the quiet halls of their home, each step a reminder of the journey they had taken together. In the comfort of their room, they settled in, grateful for the life they had built, for the love they shared, and for the promise of another day to make a difference.

Brad Jacobs, a titan of industry, a visionary entrepreneur, a devoted family man, and a philanthropist, had realized that the true measure of a life well-lived was not in the accolades and achievements but in the positive impact one leaves on the world and the people in it. His story, a blend of ambition, resilience, and compassion, would continue to inspire and guide, a beacon for those who dare to dream and strive to make those dreams a reality.

As dawn broke, casting its first gentle light through the curtains of their bedroom, Brad and Lamia Jacobs were greeted by the familiar chorus of birds, a daily reminder of the beauty and resilience of nature. These mornings were a time for reflection and gratitude, a quiet space before the day's activities began.

Brad, ever the early riser, would often take this time to stroll through the gardens, a practice that had become a form of meditation for him. The gardens, meticulously cared for, were a source of pride and joy. Each plant, each pathway, had a story, a memory attached to it - celebrations, family gatherings, quiet afternoons spent in contemplation. This connection to nature had grown stronger over the years, grounding him in the present and reminding him of life's simple pleasures.

In these morning walks, Brad often thought about the broader impact of his work. He pondered over the businesses he had built and led, the jobs created, the services provided, and the innovations spurred. He wondered about the lives he had touched, directly and indirectly, and hoped that his efforts had contributed positively to their stories.

As dawn broke, casting its first gentle light through the curtains of their bedroom, Brad and Lamia Jacobs were greeted by the familiar chorus of birds, a daily reminder of the beauty and resilience of nature. These mornings were a time for reflection and gratitude, a quiet space before the day's activities began.

Brad, ever the early riser, would often take this time to stroll through the gardens, a practice that had become a form of meditation for him. The gardens, meticulously cared for, were a source of pride and joy. Each plant, each pathway, had a story, a memory attached to it - celebrations, family gatherings, quiet afternoons spent in contemplation. This connection to nature had grown stronger over the years, grounding him in the present and reminding him of life's simple pleasures.

In these morning walks, Brad often thought about the broader impact of his work. He pondered over the businesses he had built and led, the jobs created, the services provided, and the innovations spurred. He wondered about the lives he had touched, directly and indirectly, and hoped that his efforts had contributed positively to their stories.

Back in the house, breakfast was a time for family. Despite their children having grown and ventured out to build their own lives, they often returned, filling the house with laughter and chatter. These gatherings were a source of immense happiness for Brad and Lamia, a time to reconnect, to share news, and to offer guidance. Brad took particular delight in his role as a grandfather, sharing stories of his youth, his business ventures, and the lessons life had taught him.

Throughout his career, Brad had faced numerous challenges and setbacks, each a learning experience, shaping him into the leader he had become. He often shared these stories with his grandchildren, not to boast of his successes, but to teach them the value of perseverance, adaptability, and moral courage. He wanted them to understand that failure was not the opposite of success, but a stepping stone towards it.

As the day progressed, Brad would often retreat to his home office, a space filled with mementos of his journey - awards, photographs, and gifts from colleagues and friends from around the world. Despite stepping back from the day-to-day operations of his businesses, he remained actively involved in strategic decision-making, mentoring young leaders, and advocating for the causes he believed in.

His work in philanthropy had expanded over the years, driven by a deep-seated desire to give back to the community that had given him so much. He focused on creating opportunities for those less fortunate, believing that everyone deserved a chance to succeed. Education, healthcare, environmental conservation, and the arts were among the key areas he supported, each reflecting a facet of his values and beliefs.

Evenings were a time for relaxation and family. Brad and Lamia often hosted friends and colleagues, their home a welcoming place for lively discussions, shared meals, and the fostering of new ideas. These gatherings were a testament to Brad's belief in the power of relationships, in the sharing of knowledge and experiences, and in the joy of bringing people together.

As night fell, Brad would often look back on the day with a sense of fulfillment. His life, a tapestry of experiences, successes, and challenges, was a testament to the power of vision, determination, and compassion. He had learned that true success was not just about building businesses and creating wealth, but about making a meaningful difference in the world, about leaving it a little better than he found it.

Brad Jacobs' journey from a young, ambitious entrepreneur to a respected business leader and philanthropist was more than a story of business acumen. It was a story of personal growth, of a relentless pursuit of excellence, and of a deep commitment to making a positive impact. His legacy, woven into the fabric of the many lives he touched, would continue to inspire and guide, a beacon for future generations of dreamers and doers. In the quiet of his home, surrounded by the memories of a life well-lived, Brad Jacobs could rest easy, knowing that his journey had been one of purpose, impact, and enduring value.

As the seasons changed, so did the rhythm of life in the Jacobs household. With the arrival of autumn, the garden that Brad cherished transformed into a palette of reds, oranges, and yellows, mirroring the changes he had witnessed in his own life. The falling leaves, a reminder of the impermanence of all things, also spoke to the beauty in change and the importance of letting go.

During these cooler days, Brad found more time to indulge in one of his passions – art. His collection, featuring works from Picasso to Lichtenstein, was not just a display of aesthetic appreciation but a reflection of his journey through life. Each piece told a story, a moment frozen in time, resonating with his experiences and dreams. He often wandered through his collection, sometimes with family, other times with guests, sharing insights and anecdotes, each painting a window into a different world.

Brad's relationship with art was not just that of a collector but also as a patron. He believed in supporting emerging artists, in the power of art to provoke thought, to challenge, and to inspire. His support for the arts extended beyond his collection, involving contributions to local galleries and community programs, especially those focused on bringing art to underprivileged communities.

In these quieter days, Brad also found more time to write. His upcoming book, "How to Make a Few Billion Dollars," was not just a business manual but a reflection on his life, his philosophies, and the principles that guided him. He hoped his book would serve as a roadmap for young entrepreneurs, a source of inspiration for those daring to dream big. The writing process was a journey in itself, an opportunity for introspection and sharing the wisdom gleaned from a lifetime of experiences.

Lamia, ever supportive, played a crucial role in this phase of Brad's life. She was his sounding board, offering insights and perspectives that enriched his writing. Their discussions often delved deep into topics of business, life, and legacy, each conversation strengthening the bond they shared.

Brad's days were also marked by his continued mentorship to young business leaders. He found great satisfaction in guiding the next generation, sharing his insights and learning from their fresh perspectives. This exchange of ideas kept him connected to the ever-evolving business landscape, a world he had helped shape but which was now being reshaped by younger minds.

Yet, even as he engaged with the world, Brad never lost sight of the importance of balance. He cherished his time with family – the quiet dinners, the weekend outings, the celebrations of milestones. These moments were his anchor, a reminder of what truly mattered.

As the years passed, Brad Jacobs' name became synonymous not just with business success but with a life lived with purpose and generosity. His story was not just one of financial success but of resilience, innovation, and a deep-seated commitment to making a positive impact.

In his twilight years, surrounded by the love of his family and the respect of his peers, Brad could look back on his life with a sense of fulfillment. He had navigated the highs and lows with grace, had stayed true to his values, and had left an indelible mark on the world. His legacy, built not just on what he had achieved but on how he had achieved it, would continue to inspire long after the sun had set on his remarkable journey. In every decision made, in every life touched, Brad Jacobs' story would continue to resonate, a testament to the enduring power of a life well-lived.

As Brad Jacobs entered the autumn of his life, he often found himself reflecting on the journey that had brought him to this point. The quiet moments were filled with memories of the challenges he'd faced, the triumphs he'd celebrated, and the myriad of lessons learned along the way. He realized that each step, whether it was a leap forward or a stumble, had shaped him into the person he was today.

One of Brad's most cherished routines was the long, reflective walks he took through the neighborhood, often accompanied by Lamia. These strolls were more than just physical exercise; they were a ritual that allowed him to connect with his community and nature, and to engage in deep conversations with his wife. They would talk about everything from their children's futures to the evolving dynamics of the global economy. Brad valued Lamia's insights immensely, often finding clarity and wisdom in her words.

In these later years, Brad also dedicated more time to philanthropic endeavors. He was particularly passionate about educational initiatives, understanding that knowledge was a key driver of social and economic progress. He set up scholarships and funded educational programs, especially in underprivileged areas, hoping to provide opportunities for those who needed them most. For Brad, the joy of giving back was not just in the act itself but in seeing the tangible impact of these initiatives on people's lives.

Brad's children, now adults with their own paths and careers, often sought his advice on various matters, from business to personal life. He was a source of wisdom, offering guidance without imposing, always encouraging them to make their own decisions and learn from their experiences. His role as a grandfather was one he cherished deeply, reveling in the simple joys of playing with his grandchildren, reading them stories, and instilling in them the values of hard work, integrity, and kindness.

Technology, a constant in Brad's business life, now played a different role. He used it to stay connected with friends, former colleagues, and family members scattered across the globe. Brad was fascinated by the ever-evolving digital landscape and often mused about the changes he had witnessed over the years, from the rise of the internet to the advent of artificial intelligence.

As Brad's legacy in the business world solidified, he found a new sense of purpose in sharing his story. He participated in interviews, gave talks at universities, and attended conferences, not to bask in his past achievements, but to inspire and empower the next generation of entrepreneurs and leaders. His message was always one of perseverance, ethical leadership, and the importance of balancing ambition with personal fulfillment.

Evenings in the Jacobs household were serene and filled with warmth. Brad and Lamia often spent their time enjoying music, a passion that had remained constant throughout Brad's life. The notes of classical compositions or the rhythms of jazz filled their home, creating an ambiance of tranquility and reflection.

Brad's life story, from a young, ambitious businessman to a respected elder with a wealth of knowledge and experience, was a tapestry of determination, innovation, and compassion. His journey was a powerful reminder that success is not measured just by what one achieves for oneself, but by what one contributes to the world. Brad Jacobs' legacy was not just in the businesses he built and the wealth he generated, but in the lives he touched, the communities he uplifted, and the positive change he inspired.

As he sat by the fireplace on a chilly evening, looking at the flames dancing and thinking about the future, Brad felt a profound sense of gratitude. He had traversed a remarkable path, one marked by both extraordinary achievements and humbling lessons. The legacy he would leave behind was a beacon for those who dared to dream, a reminder that with vision, hard work, and a heart for giving, one could indeed make a significant impact on the world. The story of Brad Jacobs was more than a tale of business success; it was a narrative of a life rich in purpose, a life that would continue to inspire and guide many, long into the future.

As Brad Jacobs entered the autumn of his life, he often found himself reflecting on the journey that had brought him to this point. The quiet moments were filled with memories of the challenges he'd faced, the triumphs he'd celebrated, and the myriad of lessons learned along the way. He realized that each step, whether it was a leap forward or a stumble, had shaped him into the person he was today.

One of Brad's most cherished routines was the long, reflective walks he took through the neighborhood, often accompanied by Lamia. These strolls were more than just physical exercise; they were a ritual that allowed him to connect with his community and nature, and to engage in deep conversations with his wife. They would talk about everything from their children's futures to the evolving dynamics of the global economy. Brad valued Lamia's insights immensely, often finding clarity and wisdom in her words.

In these later years, Brad also dedicated more time to philanthropic endeavors. He was particularly passionate about educational initiatives, understanding that knowledge was a key driver of social and economic progress. He set up scholarships and funded educational programs, especially in underprivileged areas, hoping to provide opportunities for those who needed them most. For Brad, the joy of giving back was not just in the act itself but in seeing the tangible impact of these initiatives on people's lives.

Brad's children, now adults with their own paths and careers, often sought his advice on various matters, from business to personal life. He was a source of wisdom, offering guidance without imposing, always encouraging them to make their own decisions and learn from their experiences. His role as a grandfather was one he cherished deeply, reveling in the simple joys of playing with his grandchildren, reading them stories, and instilling in them the values of hard work, integrity, and kindness.

In the quiet twilight of his career, Brad Jacobs found a unique kind of peace, a harmony that came with the understanding that his life's work had transcended mere business achievements. The long evenings at home were often spent in the company of old friends and new acquaintances, sharing stories that were a tapestry of experiences, laughter, lessons, and wisdom.

Brad's home, filled with the art he had collected over the years, stood not just as a residence but as a testament to his journey. Each piece of art, each sculpture, and painting, was a chapter of his life, a reminder of a particular period, challenge, or triumph. These were more than just investments; they were the silent witnesses to his life's story.

The Jacobs family gatherings were lively affairs, brimming with energy and love. Brad took great pride in seeing his children and grandchildren interact, each carrying a part of his legacy in their own unique way. He often shared stories of his early ventures, not just to entertain but to impart lessons that he hoped would guide them through their own challenges.

As an elder statesman in the business community, Brad's counsel was sought by many. He served on advisory boards, not just lending his expertise but also learning and staying abreast of the latest trends and technologies. He was particularly intrigued by the advancements in sustainable practices and often advocated for responsible and ethical business strategies.

Brad also spent time nurturing his personal passions. His love for music, which had been a constant companion throughout his life, now took on a new dimension. He sponsored local music festivals and supported young musicians, providing them with the platforms to showcase their talents. His belief in the power of music to unite and heal was evident in his unwavering support for these initiatives.

With Lamia by his side, Brad traveled, not for business, but for pleasure and exploration. They visited places that had been on their wish list for years, experiencing different cultures, cuisines, and landscapes. These travels were not just leisurely escapades but journeys of discovery, as each destination offered new perspectives and insights.

In his quieter moments, Brad took to writing not just about business, but about life itself. He penned essays and reflections, sharing his thoughts on various subjects from leadership and ethics to family and aging. These writings were cherished by his readers, offering glimpses into the mind of a man who had navigated the complexities of life with grace and resilience.

Brad's philanthropic efforts continued to expand. He was particularly passionate about environmental conservation, understanding the critical need to preserve the planet for future generations. His investments in green technologies and initiatives to combat climate change were not just about philanthropy but about legacy – a commitment to leaving the world a better place.

As Brad looked back on his life, he realized that his truest legacy was not in the businesses he built or the wealth he accumulated, but in the lives he touched and the positive changes he inspired. His journey was a testament to the belief that true success comes from the impact one has on the world and the people around them.

In the golden years of his life, surrounded by the love of his family and the respect of his peers, Brad Jacobs stood as a beacon of integrity, innovation, and philanthropy. His story was not just one of business acumen but of a life richly lived, a life that would continue to inspire and guide others towards their own paths of success and fulfillment. Brad Jacobs, a businessman, a family man, a mentor, and a philanthropist, had indeed written a story worth telling, a story that would endure as a legacy for generations to come.

As autumn turned to winter, Brad Jacobs found himself in a reflective mood, often gazing out at the snow-blanketed landscape from his study, a room lined with books and memories. He pondered over the intricate tapestry of life, how each thread – every decision, every risk taken, and every obstacle overcome – had contributed to the rich pattern of his existence.

During these contemplative hours, Brad found solace in writing letters. In an age dominated by digital communication, he cherished the personal touch of handwritten notes. He wrote to friends, former colleagues, and even to those young entrepreneurs who sought his mentorship, imparting wisdom in each carefully penned word. These letters were not just messages; they were pieces of himself, imbued with experience and sincerity.

The holiday season was a special time in the Jacobs household. It was an occasion that brought the extended family together, filling the home with laughter, stories, and the warmth of shared love. Brad, with his ever-present twinkle of joy, would orchestrate the festivities, ensuring that each family member felt the special magic of the season. It was during these gatherings that Brad's role as the patriarch was most evident, as he shared tales of past Christmases, each story a lesson wrapped in nostalgia.

Brad's involvement in community affairs deepened. He regularly attended local council meetings, offering insights and support to local initiatives. His business acumen, coupled with his genuine concern for community welfare, made him a respected figure in these circles. Brad understood that true change often began at the grassroots level, and he was committed to playing a part in shaping the community for the better.

Brad and Lamia also found joy in their shared hobby of gardening, an interest that had grown over the years. Their garden was a place of tranquility and beauty, a testament to their teamwork and dedication. It became a sanctuary where they could both work and relax, surrounded by the blooms and scents of the seasons. Gardening taught Brad patience and the importance of nurturing, lessons he applied in all aspects of his life.

In his philanthropic endeavors, Brad was particularly focused on creating sustainable impacts. He launched initiatives aimed at empowering young entrepreneurs, especially those from underprivileged backgrounds. He believed in giving people the tools to build their futures, whether through education, mentorship, or financial support. Brad knew that each individual empowered was a step towards a better world.

Despite his successes and the accolades he had received, Brad remained humble. He often said that his greatest achievements were not the companies he built or the deals he closed, but the moments of quiet kindness, the opportunities to help others grow, and the joy of seeing those he loved flourish.

As the years passed, Brad Jacobs's legacy continued to grow, not just in the business world but in the hearts and lives of those he touched. His journey was a beacon of hope and inspiration, a reminder that one's life is not measured by material success alone, but by the depth of one's character and the impact one has on others. Brad Jacobs, a man of vision, integrity, and compassion, had indeed written a story for the ages, a story of a life well-lived and a world positively changed.

The twilight years of Brad Jacobs' life were a period of graceful aging, filled with the satisfaction of past achievements and the quiet joy of present moments. His days were a blend of leisure and continued engagement with the world he had helped shape. Each morning, he would sit in his favorite armchair, often with a cup of coffee, looking out at the garden that he and Lamia had tenderly cultivated. The garden, with its thriving plants and vibrant colors, was a metaphor for his life — carefully nurtured, resilient, and full of beauty.

Brad's role as a mentor took on new dimensions. He started hosting informal gatherings at his home for young entrepreneurs and business leaders. These sessions, fondly called "Brad's Fireside Chats," became a coveted invitation in business circles. Seated by the fireplace in his expansive living room, Brad shared stories, insights, and advice, fostering a sense of community and mutual learning among the next generation of leaders.

His philanthropic efforts, too, continued unabated. Brad established scholarships for promising students in the fields of business, mathematics, and music, reflecting the diverse interests that had shaped his own life. He also funded research initiatives in environmental sustainability, passionate about contributing to a greener future.

Brad's relationship with his wife, Lamia, deepened further in these years. They were companions in the truest sense, sharing interests, supporting each other's endeavors, and finding new adventures together. They traveled, but more selectively now, preferring destinations that offered serene beauty and a rich cultural tapestry. These travels were no longer about exploration but about savoring the experiences and creating lasting memories.

The bonds with his children and grandchildren were sources of immense joy for Brad. He took great pride in their accomplishments, whether in academics, careers, or personal milestones. His guidance was always a blend of wisdom and encouragement, urging them to pursue their passions and make meaningful contributions to the world.

Brad's health, though generally good, began to demand more attention with age. He faced these challenges with the same resilience and positive attitude that had characterized his approach to life's earlier obstacles. His physical limitations did not dampen his spirit; instead, they provided him with more time for reflection and writing.

In these later years, Brad penned a memoir, an intimate account of his journey through life's ups and downs. The memoir was more than just a chronicle of his business achievements; it was a narrative of personal growth, relationships, and his philosophical outlook on life. The book received critical acclaim, celebrated for its honesty, wisdom, and the inspiring story it told.

As Brad Jacobs looked back on his life, he saw a path marked by ambition, resilience, and the pursuit of excellence. But more importantly, he saw a life rich in relationships, learning, and giving back. He had lived not just for himself but for the betterment of others, leaving a legacy that would inspire and impact many generations.

In the quiet evenings of his later years, sitting by the fireplace and surrounded by the love of his family, Brad Jacobs could look back with contentment at a life well-lived. His story was not just one of success in the traditional sense but a testament to the power of perseverance, kindness, and a deep commitment to making a positive difference in the world.

As the seasons continued their eternal cycle, Brad Jacobs found himself increasingly introspective, often taking long walks through the garden with Lamia, reflecting on the journey of life. These walks were times of silent communion with nature and each other, punctuated by conversations about the past, musings about the future, and observations of the ever-changing landscape around them.

Brad's role as a patriarch and mentor extended beyond his immediate family and business circles. He became a revered figure in his community, someone people looked up to for guidance and inspiration. His home, with its welcoming warmth and walls adorned with art that told stories of history and creativity, became a hub for gatherings – not just of business minds but of artists, musicians, and local leaders. Brad believed in the power of diverse perspectives and the magic that ensued when different worlds collided and collaborated.

In his community, Brad initiated and supported various cultural and artistic endeavors. He funded local art programs, believing that creativity was a crucial component of a vibrant community. He also sponsored music festivals and art exhibitions, providing platforms for local talents to showcase their work and for the community to celebrate its cultural richness.

Brad's passion for music, a constant companion throughout his life, found new expression in these years. He took up playing the piano again, an activity he had set aside in the whirlwind of his business career. The music room in their home, with its grand piano and walls lined with shelves of classical and jazz records, became a sanctuary where Brad would spend hours rediscovering his musical talents.

The legacy of Brad's business acumen continued to thrive. The companies he had founded and nurtured were now in the hands of competent leaders, many of whom he had personally mentored. These businesses continued to innovate and grow, each a testament to Brad's vision and leadership. His role had evolved from active management to that of an esteemed advisor, offering wisdom gleaned from decades of experience.

Brad and Lamia's golden anniversary was a celebration that brought together friends, family, and associates from all walks of life. It was a festive event, reflecting the couple's journey together – a blend of love, partnership, and shared dreams. Their children and grandchildren, each a unique blend of the couple's values and traits, were a source of immense pride and joy.

In his quieter moments, Brad took to writing letters to his grandchildren, imparting lessons and stories from his life. These letters, written with love and care, were his way of ensuring that the wisdom of his experiences would be passed down through generations.

As the twilight of his life drew near, Brad looked at his legacy with a sense of fulfillment. He had not only built successful businesses but had also invested in people and communities, nurturing growth, innovation, and creativity. His life was a tapestry of achievements, not measured in monetary terms but in the richness of experiences and the positive impact he had on others.

Brad Jacobs' story is a testament to the power of vision, resilience, and compassion. His journey from a curious, music-loving youth to a revered business leader and community pillar was marked by his unwavering commitment to making a difference in every facet of life. His legacy, woven through the lives of those he touched, stood as a beacon of inspiration, a reminder that the true measure of success lies in the depth of one's impact on the world and the people around them.

As the final chapters of Brad Jacobs' life unfolded, he found himself reflecting on the impermanence of existence and the enduring nature of the impacts we leave behind. With Lamia by his side, his home filled with the laughter of grandchildren, and his professional legacy secure, Brad turned his attention to encapsulating his life's philosophy and wisdom for future generations.

The Jacobs family home, a testament to Brad's life journey, became a place of gathering and celebration, where the values of hard work, integrity, and kindness were palpably felt. The walls, adorned with masterpieces from Picasso to Calder, were not just displays of aesthetic brilliance but symbols of Brad's belief in the transformative power of art. The art collection, carefully curated over decades, was not only a source of personal joy but also a legacy he planned to leave for the public. Discussions were underway to donate a significant portion of it to art museums, ensuring that these treasures could be enjoyed and appreciated by a broader audience.

Brad's philanthropic efforts, already significant, took on a new dimension. He established a foundation focused on supporting education, the arts, and environmental sustainability, causes close to his heart. The foundation, led by a team of dedicated professionals and guided by Brad's vision, worked to create opportunities for underprivileged youth, foster artistic talent, and promote sustainable business practices.

In the realm of business, Brad continued to be a figure of immense respect and influence. Though no longer involved in day-to-day operations, his advice was sought by industry leaders and young entrepreneurs alike. His approach to business, always ahead of its time, continued to be studied in business schools around the world. The principles he espoused – ethical leadership, customer-centric services, and innovation – had become integral parts of modern business education.

Brad's autobiography, a blend of personal anecdotes and professional wisdom, became a bestseller, resonating with people from all walks of life. He followed it with a series of lectures at universities, business forums, and public events, sharing his insights on life, leadership, and the pursuit of meaningful success. These talks, often interspersed with his characteristic humor and humility, were a source of inspiration for many.

As age advanced, Brad and Lamia's world became smaller but no less rich. Their home, a hub of activity in the past, now became a sanctuary of peace and reflection. The couple, always avid readers, spent hours in their library, immersed in the world of books. Their evenings were often spent listening to music, the notes of jazz and classical pieces filling their home with a sense of serenity and contentment.

Brad's health, while fragile, did not dampen his spirit. He faced his physical limitations with grace and acceptance, using this time to connect more deeply with his inner self and with those he loved. Conversations with his children and grandchildren became more profound, often touching on the themes of life, love, and legacy. He encouraged them to live lives of purpose, to seek happiness in relationships and experiences, and to contribute positively to the world.

In his final days, surrounded by his family, Brad Jacobs was a picture of contentment and peace. His life had been a remarkable journey of transformation – from a young man with dreams of music and mathematics to a business titan who changed the face of several industries. More than his business acumen, it was his humanity, his unwavering commitment to bettering the lives of others, and his deep appreciation for the beauty of life that defined him.

Brad Jacobs passed away leaving a legacy that transcended his business achievements. His was a life that exemplified the belief that true success is about enriching the world and touching lives. He left behind not just a thriving business empire and a remarkable collection of art but, more importantly, a family imbued with his values and countless individuals inspired by his life's story. Brad Jacobs' journey, marked by its triumphs, challenges, and unwavering humanity, would continue to inspire and guide generations to come.

As the world mourned the loss of Brad Jacobs, his legacy continued to reverberate far beyond the walls of his home and the companies he had built. His passing was not just the end of a life but the beginning of a legacy that would inspire countless others.

In Greenwich, Connecticut, where Brad and Lamia had spent much of their lives, the impact of his passing was palpable. The community, which had benefited from his generosity and vision, came together to honor him. A memorial service was held, not in a traditional setting, but at the local art museum, a place that had flourished partly due to Brad's patronage. People from all walks of life – business leaders, artists, local residents – gathered to pay their respects. The walls of the museum, adorned with pieces from Brad's collection, served as a fitting backdrop, a silent testament to his love for art and his belief in its power to inspire and transform.

The memorial service was a tapestry of music, art, and heartfelt tributes. Friends and family shared stories – some poignant, some humorous – of Brad's life and the countless ways he had touched their lives. A local jazz band, one of the many art initiatives Brad had supported, played his favorite pieces, filling the space with melodies that Brad had so dearly loved.

In the days following his passing, Brad's foundation announced a series of initiatives in his honor. These included scholarships for students pursuing careers in business and the arts, grants for environmental sustainability projects, and a program to support emerging artists. Brad's belief in giving back to the community and nurturing future generations was now being carried forward with renewed vigor.

Brad's businesses, each a leader in its respective industry, continued to operate on the principles he had instilled. The CEOs of XPO Logistics, GXO Logistics, and RXO, along with United Rentals, organized a joint conference to honor Brad's legacy in the business world. They announced the establishment of an annual leadership summit in his name, aimed at fostering innovation and ethical business practices.

Made in United States
Orlando, FL
20 March 2025